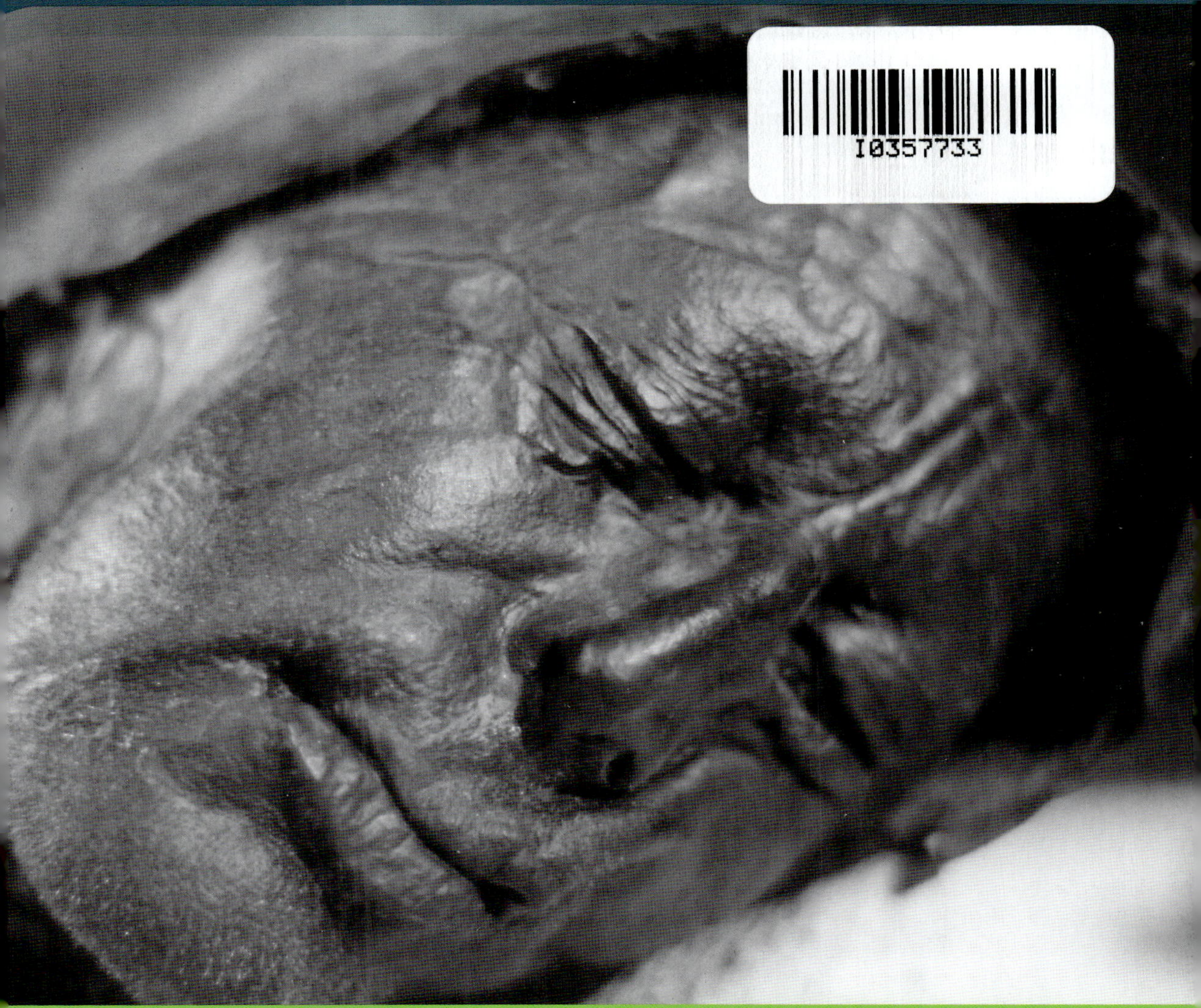

12 SUSPENSEFUL MYSTERIES

by Samantha S. Bell

STORY LIBRARY
MORE TO EXPLORE

www.12StoryLibrary.com

Copyright © 2020 by 12-Story Library, Mankato, MN 56002. All rights reserved. No part of this book may be reproduced or utilized in any form or by any means without written permission from the publisher.

12-Story Library is an imprint of Bookstaves.

Photographs ©: Sven Rosborn/PD, cover, 1; PD, 4; PD, 5; Grönneger 1/CC3.0, 6; Wikimol/CC3.0, 7; Richard McCully/PD, 8; NormanEinstein/CC3.0, 8; US National Archives and Records Administration/PD, 9; CC3.0, 9; Lt. Comdr. Horace Bristol, US Navy/PD, 10; WindVector/Shutterstock.com, 10; PD, 11; Giuseppe Enrie, 1931/PD, 12; Secundo Pia/PD, 13; PD, 14; User: SnowFire/CC4.0, 14; Harris & Ewing/Library of Congress, 15; Sam Fentress/CC2.0, 16; Saunders/PD, 16; George Grie/CC4.0, 18; Dimitrios/Shutterstock.com, 19; PD, 19; Chronicle/Alamy Stock Photo, 20; Chronicle/Alamy Stock Photo, 21; PD, 22; Denys/CC3.0, 22; Maksimilian/Shutterstock.com, 23; US Federal Government/PD, 24; US Federal Bureau of Investigation/PD, 24; FBI/PD, 25; Durbed/CC3.0, 26; edeantoine/Shutterstock.com, 27; Osama Shukir Muhammed Amin FRCP/CC4.0, 28; ducu59us/Shutterstock.com, 29

ISBN
9781632357397 (hardcover)
9781632358486 (paperback)
9781645820253 (ebook)

Library of Congress Control Number: 2019938678

Printed in the United States of America
July 2019

About the Cover
The bog body of a man known as Tollund Man, discoverd in Tollund, Denmark, in 1950.

Access free, up-to-date content on this topic plus a full digital version of this book. Scan the QR code on page 31 or use your school's login at 12StoryLibrary.com.

Table of Contents

The *Mary Celeste*: Lost at Sea 4

Bog Bodies: Perfect Corpses 6

Oak Island: Buried Treasure 8

Bermuda Triangle: Deadly Seas 10

The Shroud of Turin: Hidden Image 12

Amelia Earhart: A Hero Vanishes 14

Nessie: Monster in the Loch 16

Atlantis: City under the Sea 18

Falcon Lake: Man Meets UFO 20

The Tunguska Event: Fire in the Sky 22

D.B. Cooper: Daring Escape 24

Mokele-Mbembe: A Dinosaur Roams the Jungle 26

More Suspenseful Mysteries 28

Glossary 30

Read More 31

Index 32

About the Author 32

The *Mary Celeste*: Lost at Sea

On November 7, 1872, a ship called the *Mary Celeste* set out from New York Harbor. The ship's captain was named Benjamin Briggs. His wife, Sarah, and two-year-old daughter, Sophia, were traveling with him. The captain's son had stayed at home in Massachusetts.

Seven crew members sailed with the family. They were headed for Genoa, Italy. The ship carried 1,701 barrels of alcohol. It would be used for fuel.

Almost a month passed. Captain David Morehouse was sailing his ship near Portugal. His crew spotted the *Mary Celeste*. Captain Morehouse

An 1861 painting of the *Mary Celeste*.

was surprised. The *Mary Celeste* should have already reached Genoa.

Morehouse sent men to search the ship. There was enough food and water to last six months. But the family and the crew had disappeared. Some of the captain's papers were missing. A lifeboat was missing, too.

No one knows why Captain Briggs left his ship. He was an experienced captain, and the ship was in good condition. Some people believe the ship was attacked by pirates. But all the cargo was still on the ship. Others think there may have been a mutiny. Another theory is that fumes from the alcohol caused a small explosion. The captain may have been worried the whole ship would blow.

Captain Benjamin Briggs, his wife Sarah, and daughter Sophia.

37
Captain Briggs's age in years when he disappeared

- In 1885, a businessman named Wesley Gove bought the *Mary Celeste*.
- He sank the ship near Haiti to get insurance money for it.
- The insurance company wasn't fooled, and Gove didn't get paid.

THINK ABOUT IT

Benjamin Briggs was a captain, a husband, and a father. He probably had to make some very difficult decisions. Describe a time when you had a hard decision to make.

2

Bog Bodies: Perfect Corpses

Tollund Man is on display at Museum Silkeborg in Demark.

Viggo Højgaard and his wife, Grethe, lived in Tollund, Denmark. In May 1950, they went with Højgaard's brother to a nearby peat bog. A peat bog is a damp, murky area. In the bog, dead plants and moss build up in thick layers. The plant remains form peat over time. Peat is burned for fuel. The Højgaard family used spades to cut the peat.

Suddenly, they struck a body. They had discovered an adult man. He had a rope around his neck. At first, they thought he was a modern murder victim. But his body looked rubbery and squashed. They called the police. The police had heard about other bodies found in the bogs. They knew this man died many years ago.

The man became known as Tollund Man. He is one of many ancient people who have been found in peat bogs. These "bog bodies" have also been discovered in Ireland and Germany. They have been found

2,300
Number of years ago Tollund Man lived

- The first recorded discovery of a bog body was in Germany in 1640.
- Hundreds of bog bodies have been discovered.
- Tollund Man is on display at Museum Silkeborg in Denmark.

MUMMIFIED UNDER MOSS

The bodies are preserved because of the peat bogs. The bogs do not contain much oxygen or minerals. But they do have a lot of acid. This keeps the bodies from decomposing. Their hair, skin, and clothes are preserved. So is the food in their stomachs. Tollund Man wore a cap and a belt.

Most of the people probably lived in the Netherlands and the United Kingdom. Bog people have included men, women, and some children. Most of the people probably lived between 500 BCE and 100 CE. Like Tollund Man, almost all appear to have been murdered. Archaeologists are still not sure where these people came from. They don't know how they lived or why they were killed.

Sphagnum moss, also called peat moss, is one of the most common components in peat.

3

Oak Island: Buried Treasure

Long ago, pirates sailed the Atlantic coast. People heard legends of their buried gold. In 1795, 16-year-old Daniel McGinnis was hunting on Oak Island near Nova Scotia, Canada. He noticed a strange dip in the ground. Part of an old ship hung above it on a tree limb. The next day, McGinnis and two friends started digging in that spot. Soon they came across a flat stone slab. As they dug down to 30 feet (9 m), they found layers of timber. But they could not go any further.

In 1803, McGinnis and two others formed a treasure hunting company. They continued to dig in the pit. At 90 feet (27 m) down, they uncovered a stone slab with strange writing. Then, at 108 feet (33 m), water filled the pit.

Since then, many other treasure hunters have searched the pit. Each time they dug down, it filled with water. Many believe it is a

An aerial view of Oak Island Money Pit in 1931.

Franklin D. Roosevelt (third from right) and team search for the treasure circa 1909.

booby trap. The pit is now 190 feet (60 m) deep, but no treasure has yet been found.

Some people think the treasure belonged to a pirate named Captain Kidd. Others think it may be the missing jewels of Queen Marie Antoinette of France. It could also be a Viking ship that was swallowed by quicksand.

6
Number of people who have died looking for the treasure

- The hole became known as the Oak Island Money Pit.
- In 1909, Franklin D. Roosevelt tried to find treasure in the pit.
- In 2014, a worker found a 17th-century Spanish coin.

FOLLOWING THE HUNTERS

Oak Island has become the subject of a TV show. The show is called *The Curse of Oak Island*. It follows brothers Rick and Marty Lagina as they search for the treasure. Rick first read about it in 1965. He was 11 years old. Since then, he has dreamed of finding it.

4
Bermuda Triangle: Deadly Seas

A flight of five Grumman TBM Avengers from 1945.

In December 1945, five US Navy planes flew over the Bermuda Triangle. The Bermuda Triangle is a 500,000 square mile (804,672 sq km) area in the Atlantic Ocean. The three points of the triangle are Puerto Rico, Miami, and Bermuda. The planes were on a training mission called Flight 19. Their leader was Lieutenant Charles Taylor. He was an experienced pilot and a war veteran.

At first, everything seemed to go smoothly. But then Taylor's compass began to malfunction. He became confused as to their location. He led Flight 19 out to sea. Their radio communication stopped. Flight 19 was never heard from again. A

THINK ABOUT IT

If the weather was good, would you be willing to travel through the Bermuda Triangle? Why or why not?

14
Number of crew members lost on Flight 19

- The Bermuda Triangle is also known as the Devil's Triangle and the Deadly Triangle.
- In the 1400s, Christopher Columbus reported strange activity in the area.
- Over the past 500 years, as many as 2,000 ships and 35 planes may have vanished there.

search party of more than 300 boats and planes could not find any trace of them.

The Bermuda Triangle is still a deadly zone for ships and planes. Some people believe the danger may be caused by the lost city of Atlantis. Others say the triangle may be a portal between galaxies. Some think aliens or sea monsters may be involved.

Some scientists now believe that conditions in the environment could explain the disappearances. Most tropical storms and hurricanes in the Atlantic pass through the Bermuda Triangle. The Gulf Stream is a strong ocean current in the area. It can also cause quick changes in the weather.

Lieutenant Charles Taylor was 28 years old when Flight 19 vanished in the Bermuda Triangle.

5 The Shroud of Turin: Hidden Image

According to the Bible, Jesus was crucified by the Romans. After he died, his followers wrapped his body in a linen cloth. In 1354, a linen burial cloth was discovered in Turkey. Many people believed it belonged to Jesus. The cloth became part of a collection of artifacts at a cathedral in Italy. It was named the Shroud of Turin.

Under normal conditions, the fabric seemed to have an image of a human body on it. There were also bloodstains on the cloth. They were in the correct places for someone who was crucified. Then, in 1898, a photographer named Secondo Pia was allowed to take photos of the cloth. Like other early photographers, he used photographic plates instead of film.

When Pia developed the plates, he saw details that weren't visible before. The plates showed the face of a man. The man had a beard and wounds. At first, some people

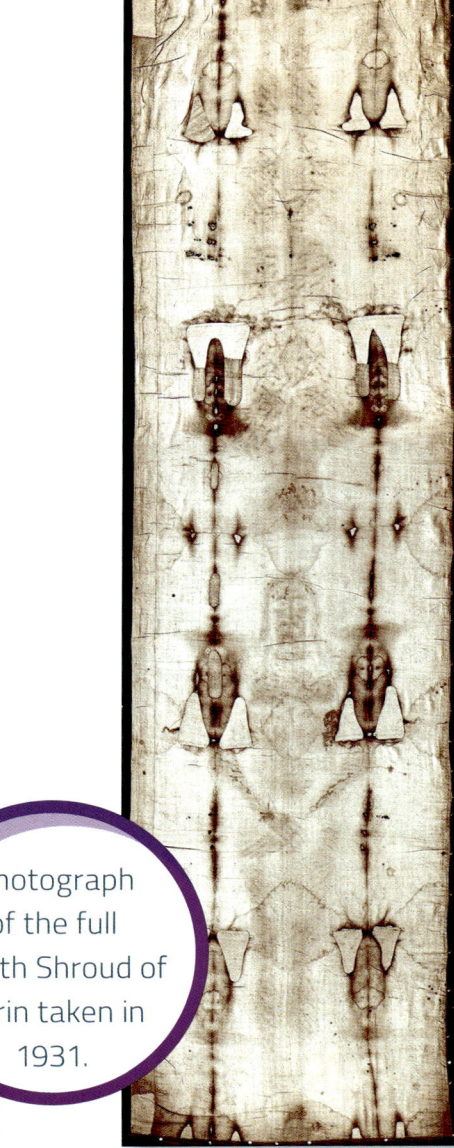

Photograph of the full length Shroud of Turin taken in 1931.

believed it was a hoax. But in the 1930s, more photos were taken. The image was still there.

Scientists were unsure about the shroud. Some believed the image had been painted onto the cloth. In 1969, they were allowed to examine the fabric. They did not find anything artificial on it. Since then, scientists have also used different methods to determine the cloth's age. They have done tests to see how the blood might have flowed onto the cloth. But they still don't have enough evidence to decide if it is real or not.

The photo of the cloth taken by Secondo Pia in 1898.

14
Length in feet (4.3 m) of the Shroud of Turin

- The Shroud of Turin was named after the cathedral in Turin, Italy, where it is kept.
- Secondo Pia was the first person to photograph the cloth.
- He used powerful electric lightbulbs to get a good image.

Amelia Earhart: A Hero Vanishes

On June 1, 1937, Earhart and her navigator, Fred Noonan, were ready to go. They took off from Miami, Florida. Along the way, they stopped in South America and Africa. Then they flew to India and New Guinea. On July 2, they headed toward Howland Island. It was more than 2,500 miles (4,023 km) away.

Earhart and Noonan check supplies next to her Electra plane on June 28, 1937.

Amelia Earhart earned her pilot's license in 1923. In 1932, she became the first woman to fly solo and nonstop across the Atlantic Ocean. Five years later, she decided to fly around world.

But Earhart and Noonan couldn't find the island. Later that day, they lost radio contact with the US Coast Guard. The Coast Guard began looking for them immediately. Nine ships and 66 airplanes also joined in the search. But Earhart and Noonan were never found.

Some people believe Earhart and Noonan crashed in the ocean. Others think the Japanese captured them. Investigators are also looking at wreckage off the coast of Buka Island near Papua New Guinea. They believe it may be Earhart's plane.

Some evidence shows that Earhart and Noonan ended up on Nikumaroro Island. After the plane disappeared, people reported hearing 57 distress calls over the radio. The speaker said she was on a small, uninhabited island. The last call came on July 7. But authorities ignored the reports.

In 1940, bones were found on Nikumaroro Island. Over the years, different scientists have studied the bones. Some say they were Earhart's, while others believe they belonged to a man. But a woman's shoe and navigation equipment were also found nearby.

Earhart in her plane in 1936.

22,000
Distance in miles (35,406 km) Earhart and Noonan covered before they disappeared

- President Franklin D. Roosevelt authorized the rescue effort.
- It cost approximately $4 million.
- Earhart was officially declared dead on January 5, 1939.

7

Nessie: Monster in the Loch

In May 1933, a couple drove along the shore of Loch Ness, a freshwater lake in Scotland. Suddenly, they saw a huge animal moving near the surface. The couple reported the sighting. The creature became known as the Loch Ness Monster, or Nessie.

That fall, several newspapers sent journalists to find the creature. In December, a big-game hunter joined the search. He didn't locate the monster. But he found footprints. One newspaper said the Loch Ness Monster was real. Many tourists went to the lake and waited for it to appear again.

The footprints turned out to be a hoax. Then, in 1934, a doctor claimed he took a photo of the monster.

This is an artist's conception of what Arthur Grant saw early one morning as he drove down a road alongside Loch Ness, Scotland. Grant dismounted and started to investigate, but the strange animal snorted and plunged into the water.

The famed photo of the Loch Ness Monster that was probably a hoax.

The picture showed a creature with a long neck rising out of the water. Many people believed the photo was real. But 60 years later, newspapers revealed it was probably a hoax, too.

Still, people keep looking for Nessie. In the 1960s, university expeditions searched the deep water using sonar. They detected a large moving object they could not explain. In 1975, scientists took photographs underwater. One seemed to show a giant flipper. The latest expeditions have not provided any better results.

800
Approximate depth in feet (244 m) of Loch Ness

- Stories of a lake monster go back to around the year 500.
- Many people claim to have seen the Loch Ness Monster.
- There have been eight official sightings.

A PLAN IN PLACE

The Scottish government has a plan in case Nessie is ever found. Scientists will take a DNA sample from the animal. Then they will release the animal back into the loch. This plan helps protect all new species found in the loch, including monsters.

8

Atlantis: City under the Sea

Artist's rendering of the Lost City of Atlantis.

The ancient Greek philosopher Plato was the first to mention Atlantis. He wrote about it around 360 BCE. Plato described the founders of Atlantis as half-human and half-god. They built their civilization on a group of islands in the Atlantic Ocean. The islands contained gold, silver, and rare wildlife. On the center island was a great capital city.

According to Plato, the people of Atlantis created a perfect society. They had an advanced culture. They had a government with a constitution. They were protected by Poseidon, the Greek god of the sea.

But as the people of Atlantis grew more powerful, they became less honorable. Their society began to fall apart. Then they sent armies to conquer parts of Africa and Europe. They went to war with the Greek city-state of Athens. Athens drove them

2
Number of Plato's writings that tell about Atlantis

- Plato said Atlantis existed about 9,000 years before his own time.
- Plato's writings are the only known records about Atlantis.
- Plato said that before him, the story was passed down by poets, priests, and others.

Statue of Plato in Athens, Greece.

back. As punishment from the gods, the island experienced earthquakes and floods. Then it sank into the sea.

Some people believe Atlantis was an actual place that was covered by the ocean. Others believe it was a continent near the Bahamas that disappeared in the Bermuda Triangle. Another theory is that the island shifted south and became Antarctica. But most historians and scientists believe Plato made it up.

BELIEVING THE STORY

The idea that Atlantis was a real place began in the late 1800s. In 1882, Ignatius Donnelly wrote a book about the accomplishments of the ancient civilizations. He said they must have learned from an earlier advanced people like those of Atlantis. He believed a continent could have flooded and sank into the ocean.

9

Falcon Lake: Man Meets UFO

Stefan Michalak was an amateur geologist. He often went looking for quartz. In May 1967, he searched the woods around Falcon Lake in Nova Scotia, Canada. While there, he noticed two bright objects in the sky. One flew away, but the other landed.

51
Michalak's age when he saw the aircraft

- The burns on Michalak's body later turned into raised sores in a grid-like pattern.
- The sores returned every few months for about a year and a half.
- Doctors could not figure out what caused the sores.

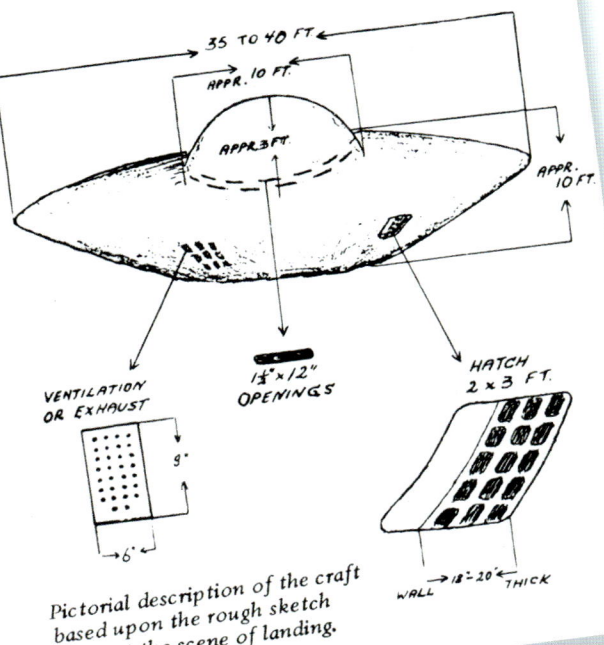

Pictorial description of the craft based upon the rough sketch made at the scene of landing.

Michalak drew a sketch of the aircraft. Then he decided to go closer. He could hear the sound of a motor and feel warm air. He heard voices inside. When he called out, the voices stopped.

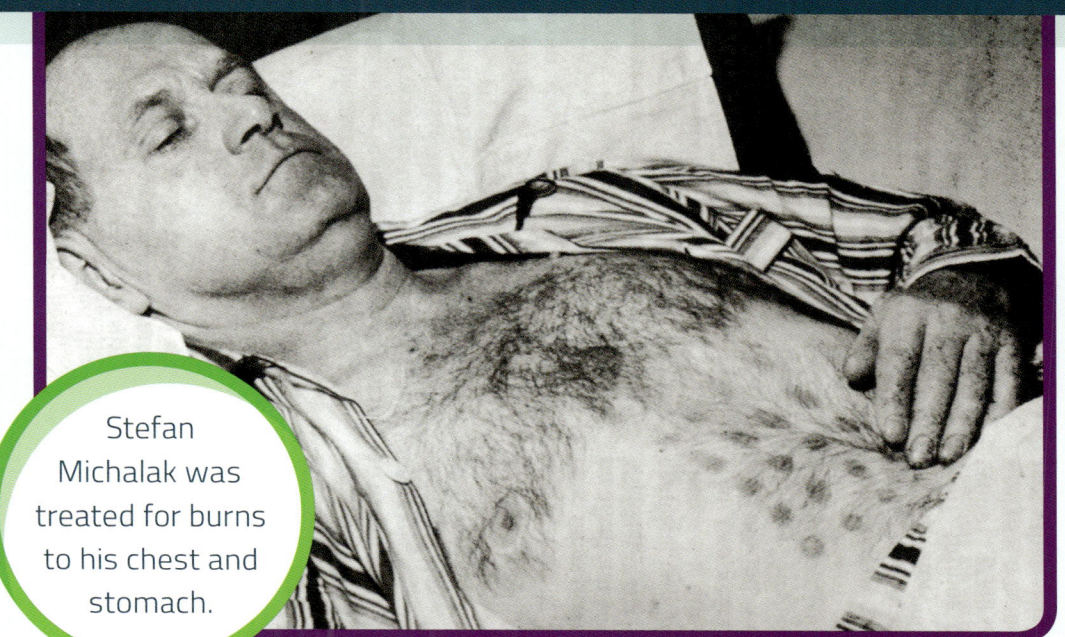

Stefan Michalak was treated for burns to his chest and stomach.

Michalak noticed an open door and looked inside. He saw panels with flashing colored lights. When he stepped away, the door closed. Michalak touched the outside of the aircraft with his glove. It was so hot it melted the fingertips.

Suddenly, the aircraft began to turn. On the side were holes that looked like a vent. A blast of hot air from the holes pushed Michalak backward. His shirt and hat caught on fire. He ripped them off as the aircraft flew away. Michalak made his way back to town and went to the hospital. He was treated for burns to his chest and stomach. He also suffered from other health problems because of the incident.

Authorities found bits of radioactive metal in the area. Some people believe it came from an alien spacecraft. Others think it was a government airship. Still others believe the whole thing was a hoax.

THINK ABOUT IT

If you had been with Michalak, would you tell people what you saw? What if they said you made it up? How would you react?

10
The Tunguska Event: Fire in the Sky

On the morning of June 30, 1908, a man was sitting on the front porch of a trading post in Siberia, Russia. Suddenly, the northern sky seemed to split in two. Over the forest, fire seemed to cover the sky. The man heard a bang followed by a huge crash. Then he heard a sound like guns firing. The earth seemed to shake. Windows smashed in. Some people felt extreme heat. Others were blown off their feet.

Forty miles (64 km) away near the Podkamennaya Tunguska River, something had hit the ground. It destroyed 800 miles (1,287 km) of forest. Eighty million trees were lying flat on the ground in a circular pattern. But the trees in the center were still standing upright. All of the bark and limbs were gone. They looked like telephone poles.

Russian newspapers reported it as a meteorite impact. But no one went to the site to investigate. Years went by. In 1921, a mineralogist named Leonid Kulik decided to lead an expedition. But harsh weather conditions held Kulik's team back. Finally, in 1927, they arrived at the site.

Zone of the meteor impact.

Artist rendering of the suspected Siberian asteroid.

After studying the area, Kulik suggested that an object from space exploded in the atmosphere. The explosion caused the fireball. Soviet scientists thought it was a comet. Some people said it was an alien spaceship crashing into the earth. Others believed the blast was a nuclear explosion. Most scientists today believe an asteroid entered the atmosphere and exploded in the sky. But more than 100 years later, they still aren't sure what caused the blast.

33,500
Estimated speed in miles per hour (53,913 km/hr) that the asteroid fell—if it was an asteroid

- The trees in the center were hit by fast-moving shock waves.
- Hundreds of reindeer were killed by the blast.
- According to records, only one person died.

11

D.B. Cooper: Daring Escape

FBI bulletin poster (above), and composite sketch of Cooper, circa 1971.

36
Number of passengers on the plane with Cooper

- A police artist made a sketch of what Cooper looked like.
- He was wearing a suit, dark sunglasses, and a thin tie.
- Suspects included former paratroopers and war veterans.

On November 24, 1971, a man who called himself Dan Cooper boarded a flight to Seattle, Washington. He was also known as D.B. Cooper. After the plane took off, he handed a note to the flight attendant. The note said he had a bomb in his briefcase.

Cooper told the flight attendant to sit beside him. He showed her the bomb. Then Cooper demanded a ransom. He wanted $200,000 in cash in $20 bills. He also wanted four parachutes. He wanted a truck ready to refuel the plane when they

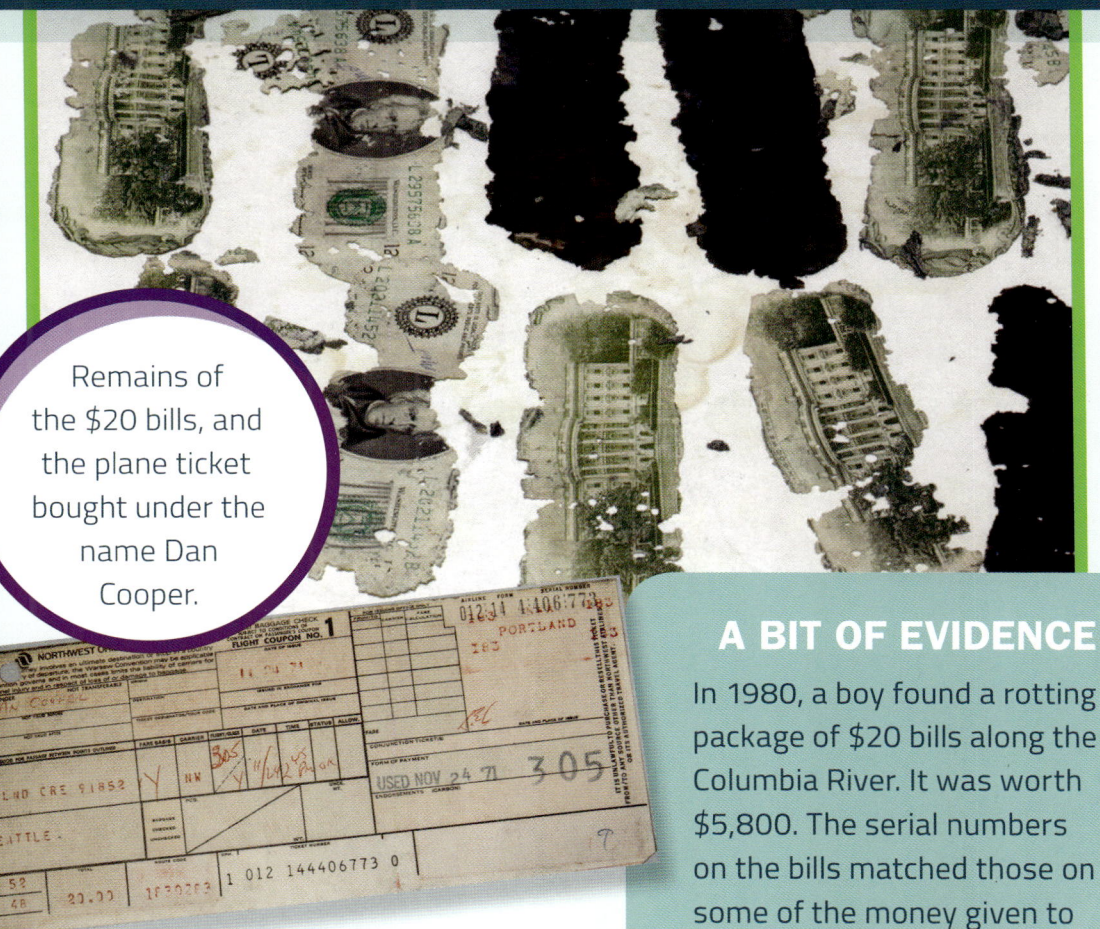

Remains of the $20 bills, and the plane ticket bought under the name Dan Cooper.

reached Seattle. The flight attendant got up to tell the captain.

In Seattle, Cooper exchanged the passengers for the money. Then he ordered the pilots to take off again. Cooper gave them a new flight plan for Mexico. He told them to keep the rear door unlocked and fly the plane low and slow. Somewhere over southwest Washington, Cooper opened the rear door and jumped. He disappeared into the night.

A BIT OF EVIDENCE

In 1980, a boy found a rotting package of $20 bills along the Columbia River. It was worth $5,800. The serial numbers on the bills matched those on some of the money given to Cooper. But in 2016, the FBI decided to stop investigating unless the parachute or more money was found.

The FBI spent years trying to find D.B. Cooper. They looked into hundreds of leads. Many people believed they knew Cooper's true identity. Others even claimed to be Cooper. But no one knows for sure who he was or what happened to him.

25

12
Mokele-Mbembe: A Dinosaur Roams the Jungle

In the late 1800s, missionaries from France traveled to the Congo region of Africa. While there, they found footprints of a large creature. The footprint was about the size of an elephant's print. But it had long claw marks. Some people believe it was made by a dinosaur species that never died out.

The dinosaur is known as the mokele-mbembe. According to the legend, the mokele-mbembe is an amphibious dinosaur with a long neck and a long tail. It is about the size of an elephant and lives near the river. Some believe it is a herbivore. But the native people say it will attack humans.

Some people do not think the mokele-mbembe is real. There are no photographs of the dinosaur. No one has found any bones or teeth. But there are many stories about it. The native people of the region are sure it exists. Some have seen its footprints. A few have even seen the dinosaur itself.

3
Number of toes on a mokele-mbembe's foot

- The mokele-mbembe is believed to be about 35 feet (11 m) long.
- Some people say it has a single horn that it uses to kill elephants.
- More than 50 expeditions have searched for the mokele-mbembe.

An artist's rendition of what a mokele-mbembe might have looked like.

THE PERFECT HABITAT FOR HIDING

The Democratic Republic of Congo is one of the few places on earth where a dinosaur could hide. The area is about 41,010 square miles (66,000 sq km) in size. According to the Congo government, about 80 percent of that is still uncharted. Much of the land is covered by a dense and often flooded forest. It is part of the second-largest rainforest in the world.

The flooded dense forest of the Congo.

More Suspenseful Mysteries

An Ancient Treasure Map
In 1952, ancient scrolls were discovered near Qumran on the shores of the Dead Sea. Most of them were made of papyrus. But one scroll was made of copper. This scroll contains a list of 64 locations, along with amounts of gold and silver. So far, no one has found the treasure.

The People of Easter Island
Easter Island is a small island about 2,300 miles (3,701.5 km) west of South America. The closest island is 1,100 miles (1,770.3 km) away. Around the year 1200, a small group of Polynesian people traveled there in wooden canoes. They created a thriving civilization. But by the time the Europeans arrived in 1722, their civilization had almost collapsed.

A strip of the copper scroll from the Qumran cave.

A Place of Secrets
Area 51 is in the Nevada desert. It is an unofficial military base. Over the years, the CIA and the Air Force used Area 51 it for experimental aircraft. Some people think it has also been used to hold aliens and their spaceships.

The Missing Lighthouse Keepers
In December 1900, James Moore sailed to the small island of Eilean Mor near Scotland. He went to the lighthouse to take the place of one of the lighthouse keepers. But the three lighthouse keepers had all left their posts. One left without his coat. They were never seen again.

Glossary

asteroid
A small, rocky object that orbits the sun.

big game
Large animals that are hunted for sport.

booby trap
A setup or device created to surprise, harm, or kill a person or an animal.

cathedral
A type of church.

crucify
To put someone to death on a cross.

comet
A small, icy object in space that has a tail made of gas and dust particles.

geologist
A scientist who studies the earth, its rocks, and how they change over time.

herbivore
An animal that eats plants.

hoax
Something false passed off as real.

mineralogist
A scientist who studies minerals and their structures.

mutiny
A rebellion against an officer in charge.

paratrooper
A person trained to jump from an airplane using a parachute.

portal
A door or passageway.

Read More

Jazynka, Kitson. *History's Mysteries: Curious Clues, Cold Cases, and Puzzles from the Past.* Washington, DC: National Geographic Kids, 2017.

Levete, Sarah. *Aliens and UFOs.* New York: Gareth Stevens Publishing, 2017.

McClellan, Ray. *The Bermuda Triangle.* Minneapolis, MN: Bellwether Media, 2014.

Owings, Lisa. *Atlantis.* Minneapolis, MN: Bellwether Media, 2014.

Skeers, Linda. *Women Who Dared: 52 Fearless Daredevils, Adventurers & Rebels.* Naperville, IL: Sourcebooks, Inc., 2017.

Visit 12StoryLibrary.com

Scan the code or use your school's login at **12StoryLibrary.com** for recent updates about this topic and a full digital version of this book. Enjoy free access to:

- Digital ebook
- Breaking news updates
- Live content feeds
- Videos, interactive maps, and graphics
- Additional web resources

Note to educators: Visit 12StoryLibrary.com/register to sign up for free premium website access. Enjoy live content plus a full digital version of every 12-Story Library book you own for every student at your school.

Index

aliens, 11, 21, 23, 29, 31
asteroid, 23, 30
Atlantis, 11, 18-19, 31

Bermuda Triangle, 10-11, 19, 31
Briggs, Benjamin, 4-5
bog bodies, 6-7

Cooper, D.B., 24-25

dinosaur, 26-27
disappear, 5, 11, 15, 19, 25

Earhart, Amelia, 14-15
expeditions, 17, 22, 26

Falcon Lake, 20-21

hoax, 13, 16-17, 21, 30

Jesus, 12-13

Loch Ness Monster, 16-17
lost, 4, 11, 14, 18-19

Mary Celeste, 4-5
Michalak, Stefan, 20-21
mokele-mbembe, 26-27

Oak Island, 8-9

Plato, 18-19

Shroud of Turin, 12-13

Taylor, Charles, 10-11
Tollund Man, 6-7
treasure, 8-9, 28
Tunguska Event, 22-23

UFO, 20-21, 31

vanish, 11, 14

About the Author
Samantha S. Bell lives in upstate South Carolina with her family and lots of animals. She is the author of more than 100 nonfiction books for children.

READ MORE FROM 12-STORY LIBRARY

Every 12-Story Library Book is available in many fomats. For more information, visit **12StoryLibrary.com**